THE LADYBIRD AND THE CENTIPEDE

The Ladybird and The Centipede

PHILIP SMITH

Contents

1
THE GREAT BALLOON

2
THE JOURNEY

3
FINDING A NEW HOME

4
AN ADVENTURE AGAIN

5
BACK TO EARTH

6
THE END OF AN ADVENTURE

7
THE STORY OF THE LADYBIRD AND THE CENTIPEDE

1

The Great Balloon

One day, a little boy called Simon was playing in the garden when he saw overhead a magnificent hot air balloon drift through the sky above his house.
Just at that moment, he had a thought. He could make his own hot air balloon! He went inside and asked his mum if he could have some money to buy a balloon. "Yes, of course" replied his mother, so off he went on his bike down to the local shops to buy a matchbox, some string and a bright red balloon.
When he returned home, Simon eagerly blew up the balloon, emptied the matchbox of all its matches and carefully made four holes, one in each side of the box. He then tied string to each of the holes and attached it to the balloon.
He took his newly constructed balloon out into the garden, but before he launched it, he realised that he would need some passengers in the balloon's matchbox basket, so he wandered down to the vegetable patch at the end of the garden and found a ladybird and a centipede sitting on a radish plant. He carefully picked them up and placed them into the matchbox.

Simon waited for a gust of wind and then let go of the balloon. The wind caught it and up - up - up it went, as high as the house!
In no time at all, the balloon was right out of sight.

2

The Journey

It was lovely inside the matchbox. There was a gentle floating sensation. 'Ffffffffffffffff' was the sound the wind made as it rushed past the balloon.
"I'm hungry!" shouted Centipede.
"Oh do be quiet, you hog!" Replied Ladybird With a frown.
Unable to think of anything nice to say to each other, they sat in silence until eventually they both went to sleep.
All night, Centipede dreamt of food and his mouth kept dribbling all over the floor.
"Don't be disgusting" yawned Ladybird, half asleep.
All of a sudden, there was a loud 'BANG!'. The red balloon had hit the branch of a tree and popped.
"What was that?" Screamed Centipede. "We're going down!"
"Help! Help!" yelled Ladybird.
Before either of them could do anything, CRASH!
They had landed in an empty field, surrounded by a few mushrooms and some rabbits grazing on the grass.
Emerging from the matchbox, Ladybird noticed that there were mushrooms growing. Knowing that mushrooms were Centipede's favourite food, she let him know.

"Where? where?" yelled Centipede, pushing past Ladybird in his excitement. Within seconds, Centipede was out of the box and stuffing his face full of as many mushrooms as he could manage in one go! "Yum yum" he seemed to mutter to himself between mouthfuls.

Ladybird got out and found a dewdrop on a blade of grass that acted as a mirror. She stared at herself and combed her hair with her left feeler. Centipede noticed what she was doing and with a mouthful of mushrooms, snorted "Don't be so vain!"

"Be quiet, I can do what I like" replied Ladybird, climbing back into the matchbox. Centipede, rather than joining her, scuttled off to pester the rabbits.

One of the rabbits kindly invited Ladybird and Centipede to share her and her babies' burrow.

"Yes please! Thank you!" replied Centipede and ran over to the matchbox to tell Ladybird the good news.

The burrow was very comfortable, full of fur and leaves. The best part was that they got to play with the little baby bunnies, who had the softest brown fur, little grey ears, a little pink tongue, two goofy white teeth and a white fluffy tail that would wiggle when they were excited.

Soon, it was night time and all the little bunnies curled up in their beds. Both Ladybird and Centipede were also tired from their big adventure, so they also curled up and joined the bunnies to go to sleep.

At about five in the morning, a fox came along and began to claw the slide of the burrow. The mother rabbit woke them all up and whispered "Quick - get further down the tunnel". In their confusion, one of the bunnies ran the wrong way towards the fox and couldn't be saved.

Ladybird and the mother rabbit burst into tears. Centipede did his best to console them, which was unusually nice of him.

While they were huddled together, cuddling, they could hear in the distance the farmer letting the cows into the field. Worried that they might get trampled on, the Ladybird suggested that they move to the next field, on the other side of the river.

"How can we cross the river?" asked Centipede.

"I don't know" replied Ladybird, "but we need to try".

Ladybird and Centipede thanked Mother Rabbit for letting them stay, giving the baby bunnies an extra hug each as they left the burrow.

When they got to the river bank, Ladybird spotted a leaf on the grass that would make a perfect little boat for them, so they climbed on board and floated over to the other side of the river.

"Oh goody!" Shouted Centipede. "There are even more mushrooms on this side!'

As soon as the leaf reached the riverbank, Centipede shot past poor Ladybird, almost knocking her into the river in his hurry to get to the mushrooms.

3

Finding a New Home

Centipede looked all around him. "Where are we going to live now?" he asked, still eating mushrooms.

"What about this empty rabbit hole?" replied Ladybird as she climbed off the leaf and onto the bank of the river.

Centipede came waddling over to inspect the burrow Ladybird had suggested. "Hmmm. Yes", he said, "This will be alright. Shall we go inside?"

The inside of the burrow was lovely. It had two separate chambers, so finally they could sleep apart. The rabbits must have only just moved out, as the burrow still felt warm.

They spent the day exploring the empty field and of course eating as many mushrooms as they could.

As the sun went down, they returned to the burrow. With full bellies, they soon both drifted off to sleep. Ladybird dreamt that she was Queen of all the insects and that Centipede was her slave and did everything that he was told.

In the morning, they ventured out of the burrow and went exploring to see what was beyond the empty field.

Ladybird found an interesting looking stick on the ground that looked a bit like a magic wand. Wishing that it was, she picked it up and wished that she had a fishing rod so that she could fish in the river. As soon as she made her wish, a fishing rod appeared in front of her. "Look!" She squealed", "my wish has come true!".

For her second wish, Ladybird wished for some matches so she could light a fire to cook the fish that she caught. For her third and last wish, she wished for millions of mushrooms for her and Centipede to eat. As soon as they appeared, Centipede was off eating as many as he could. "Leave some for me - I'm the one that wished for them after all" complained Ladybird.

When they had both eaten their fill of mushrooms, they continued on with their exploring. Just near where all the mushrooms were growing was a big hole. Feeling adventurous, they decided to climb in.

The ground inside the hole was very slippery, like a slide, and before they knew it, they were both sliding through the dark until light appeared at the end of the tunnel and they landed in a heap on the sand.

"You've ruined my hat" complained Centipede, his brim all crumpled.

Ladybird was too distracted to notice that she had landed on Centipede, as when she looked up, she noticed that they were standing on a beautiful beach surrounded by a blue sea.

"What a surprise! Isn't it wonderful - we are at the seaside!" said Ladybird, but Centipede, having already moved on from his hat being crumpled, was busy eating again.

"Look Ladybird - the sand is made of sugar, the sea is blue lemonade and the seaweed is actually green candy!" Centipede said, with a mouthful of sand spraying everywhere. "I could eat this forever!"

Ladybird walked into the sea, tasting it as she did. Centipede followed, gulping as much as he could. Before they knew it they were swimming underwater surrounded by the most magical-looking sea creatures, all made of the most delicious sweets. It was heaven!

After about ten minutes of swimming, they came across an old Catfish who was selling Sea Horses to ride on. They each bought one and climbed on. Centipede called his 'Woggle Toggle' which was the most unusual name he could think of. Ladybird called hers Sarah-Sea Horse.

Centipede decided he would lead the way, even though he didn't know where he was going.

Two hours later, when Ladybird had finally caught up, they arrived at a beautiful Treasure Island, surrounded by golden coloured sand, with huge palm trees and tropical looking flowers growing in the middle.

They got off their Sea Horses, tethered them to a nearby sea urchin and swam ashore.

"Oh look! There is a cave behind those palm trees" said Ladybird.

Before she had finished her sentence, Centipede had rushed off and was climbing the trunk of a palm tree to get to the coconuts. Being greedy and trying to get all of them at once, Centipede slipped and dropped two of the coconuts, just missing Ladybird.

With Centipede still up the tree, Ladybird walked into the cave and was met with the most incredible sight - the cave was FULL of gold coins, sparkling diamonds and rubies!

"Quickly come and see" she called to Centipede, who shimmied down the trunk.

"What is it now?" He asked, annoyed that she had distracted him from his eating.

"Look for yourself! Millions of diamonds, rubies and gold coins!"

Centipede ran in, not believing what Ladybird had told him. "My goodness! - you're actually right for once" he proclaimed.

"I'm always right" replied Ladybird whist picking up handfuls of gold and diamonds. "Anyway, let's go in further and try and find even more!"

They both wandered further down into the cave. In front of them in the distance, Centipede could see a flickering light. He ran ahead and saw that the passageway was lit by golden rain candles, that spurted out red marshmallow as they burned.

Centipede couldn't get enough of the marshmallow, which was far more exciting to him than finding more treasures.

Ladybird had a job trying to locate Centipede in the dark, but managed to find him from the loud lapping noise he was making whist eating the marshmallow.

Having got his fill of food and without waiting for Ladybird, Centipede ran further down the passage when he suddenly came to a stop, as there in front of him was a huge Merman. Ladybird caught up and hid behind him. "Shhhhhhhhhhh" said Centipede, turning to her, but it was too late, the Merman had spotted them and was yelling for his guards to capture them.

A school of sharks came racing through the cave and took Ladybird and Centipede into a dungeon and locked them in.

When the sharks swam away, led by the mean Merman, Centipede cried out "What are we going to do?"

Ladybird was too busy crying to answer him. She was in floods of tears at the thought of being locked in a small space with Centipede.

As Centipede swam over to comfort her, he spotted a small crack in the wall of the dungeon. He managed to squeeze through but Ladybird's shell was too big for her to fit properly. With one big push, Centipede managed to push her through the crack, but in doing so, scraped her beautiful shiny shell.

They both swum up to the surface as quickly as they could and took a big gulp of the blue lemonade sea, but instead of being sweet and fizzy, it was all salty and yuck.

They managed to swim to shore and walked up the beach to a big grassy field. In the corner of the field was a farm. They decided that they would head over to the farm to see if it would be a suitable place to sleep.

Soon after arriving, they had made friends with all the farm animals. Whilst Ladybird looked around the barns, Centipede had an egg fight with a very naughty chick who had stolen some eggs from the Mother Hen.

That night, they slept in an old cow shed in the soft hay.

In the middle of the night, Centipede woke up starving hungry. He wandered out of the barn and looked for mushrooms to eat. While he was picking them he came across a Fairy Ring of mushrooms, where several mushrooms were growing in a perfect circle.

Centipede had heard that whenever you found a Fairy Ring of mushrooms, you should make a wish that night before you go to sleep.

He wished that he could go into space and play on the moon, as he had heard that it was made of cheese.

No sooner as he had made his wish he found himself on the moon! It was like a dream come true. He felt like he was King of the World from up there - in fact, King of the Universe! He wished Ladybird could see him right now.

It was very hard to walk about the moon, as he kept floating up into space. He really had to hold onto the cheese surface tightly otherwise he would float away completely.

After a few hours, he was feeling tired and full of all the cheese he had eaten. He wondered how he would get back down to earth. Jumping seemed the best option, well, the only option really, so that's what he did.

After falling for what seemed like an eternity, he landed safely on a big pile of soft hay, right next to Ladybird, who was still fast asleep.

Centipede was so excited about his adventure to the moon that he tried to wake Ladybird to tell her. He was worried that if he waited until morning, he would just think that he had dreamt it and that he didn't really meet the Man in the Moon and eat his cheese!

It was no good. Ladybird was in too deep a sleep to be woken, so Centipede closed his eyes and he too went to sleep with his belly full of the most delicious cheese.

4

An Adventure Again

Standing over Ladybird as she snored into the hay, Centipede yelled "Wake up sleepy head! Time for another adventure!"

"What? This early in the morning? I haven't even woken up properly yet" cried Ladybird, rubbing her eyes with her feelers.

Once Ladybird had properly woken up, they headed away from the barn and back down to the beach.

Standing on the beach, eating an ice cream was Simon, the boy who had made the hot air balloon. "Look, there's the boy who put us in the matchbox" said Ladybird. "Let's ask him if he can take us back to where we belong" replied Centipede.

They approached the boy and tapped him on his toe. "Uh-hmm" started Centipede. Simon looked down to see where the sound was coming from. "Excuse me, do you remember us? We are the creatures that you put in a matchbox attached to the red balloon"

"Why yes, I do. How did you get all the way here in France?" replied Simon.
"Oh, it's a long story! It started when…"
Just as Centipede was about to start his story, Simon's mother called out for him to get back in the car as the ferry was coming.
"Ok Mum" he said.
"But what about us? - You can't leave us here!" said Centipede.
"OK, get in my pocket for now" said Simon as he picked them both up.
When they got on the ferry, Simon asked his parents if he could go out on deck and watch the waves. "Yes but be careful" replied his Dad.

On the deck, Simon reached into his pocket and pulled out the Ladybird and the Centipede. He couldn't believe that the two little creatures he had put in the matchbox all that time ago were back here with him.
Eventually, the White Cliffs of Dover came into sight and got closer and closer until the ferry had docked and it was time to get off.
It was a shame, as Ladybird and Centipede had enjoyed their boat ride, and also because their adventure was coming to an end.
On the drive back home, the car got a flat tyre, so they had to stop. Simon got out to watch his Dad change it. As he bent down to pick up the spare tyre, the Ladybird and Cen-

tipede fell out of his pocket and onto the road.
They began to call for Simon to let him know what had happened, but it was too late. Simon's Dad had fixed the tyre and Simon was back in the car and driving off.

Ladybird and Centipede stood as they watched the back of the car disappear into the distance. "Well, I must say, that wasn't very nice, getting out of that barbaric machine, dropping us on the ground and then driving off like that!" complained Centipede.
"It might have been an accident" said Ladybird in a sympathetic voice.
"Well, even so, they should have been more careful. Now we will have to find our own way back home" said Centipede.
They began the long walk along the road when Ladybird spotted a discarded matchbox laying in the gutter. "Wait! I know, we can make our own flying machine and fly home" she said excitedly.

She picked up two leaves and stuck them either side of the box to make wings and Centipede found four old drink bottle lids to make wheels out of.

They climbed inside and began to madly flap the leaf wings while Centipede pushed them along with one of his many legs. Before they knew it, they had taken off and were gliding over a corn field that was glistening like gold as the ears of corn blew gently in the wind.

It was a lovely sight looking down on all the houses and gardens as they flew through the air.

Suddenly, the sky began to darken and big dark clouds came rolling in until before they knew it, it was completely dark, like someone had turned out the lights. Everything went quiet until the clouds began to part again and made way for a beautiful salmon pink sky, like the most perfect sunset you had ever seen. They were no longer flying, but instead on a soft pink cloud, made entirely of candy floss.

"Where are we now?" they both asked.

Centipede, who couldn't contain his excitement at being surround by lollies again, leapt out of the matchbox and went for a walk to explore.

The trees were made of chocolate and mint, the flowers out of marzipan and the water in the pond was strawberry milkshake. This was surely a dream? Everything he saw was either made of sweets or delicious drinks.

The Centipede was in his glory and all he did was eat.

"This is all very nice, but it's not exactly where we were going'" said Ladybird. "We can't stay, we will have to go home" she said seriously.

"Forget home! You wouldn't find this place in a holiday brochure. I'm staying!" said Centipede.

Just at that moment, a small creature came out of a honeycomb bush and approached them.

"Hayoo! My name is Hosetoes" said the strange creature.

"Err, hello. I'm Centipede and this is my friend Ladybird".

When Hosetoes noticed Centipede's many legs, he got scared and ran away, but was soon replaced by a large shiny brass clockwork robot.

"Sorry about my Master, Hosetoes" said the robot". "He scares very easily. My name is Ella-Ka-Toot. What are your names?"

Ladybird and Centipede introduced themselves to the robot. "So, you are Earthlings then? Welcome to the Land of Tinglesway".

Ella-Ka-Toot started to make beeping sounds and out of all the flowers and trees came lots of different coloured creatures to greet Ladybird and Centipede.

As soon as they had introduced themselves, the coloured creatures all skipped back into the trees and flowers. It was all very strange.

As they stood looking at each other and wondering what on earth was going on, Ella-Ka-Toot abruptly turned around and without a word, marched away.

The light began to fade, and Ladybird and Centipede were getting sleepy again, so they snuggled into the candy floss and drifted off to sleep.

When the sun came up the next morning, everywhere was completely different. Instead of being all bright colours and sweets, it was just black, grey and brown.

It was no longer sunny, but raining from a dark grey sky. The trees looked dead and the flowers all wilted. Everything was lifeless.

"Oh, I don't like it here anymore" said Ladybird. Centipede

agreed. They decided to look for their flying machine so they could leave.

On their way to look for the flying machine, they were startled by a loud 'BOOM', followed by a bright flash of light. In front of them stood two large monsters.

"I am Thunder and I create all the storms in the sky" said the first monster. "And I am Bright-Spark" said the second monster. "I create all the lightning in the sky".

"Oh, it's err, it's.....nice to meet you both" said Ladybird. Centipede nodded. They were relieved that finally they had come across people who could help them get home, but with another loud boom and a flash of light, the monsters disappeared.

Once again, Ladybird and Centipede were all alone.

They searched for what seemed like days for their aircraft, without any luck until one morning when they were out searching, it became very dark again, just like night time, but it was still early morning.

A few hours past until darkness finally faded away and the sun began to shine. In front of them the flowers and trees were back, and there was their flying machine right under their noses.

Before they knew it, they were airborne and finally on their way home again.

As they flew off, Tinglesway grew further and further away into the distance until it was just a small pink blob.

In front of them was Earth. Soon, they would be home at last!

5

Back to Earth

Earth became bigger and bigger the closer they got until 'BUMP', suddenly they crash landed in the middle of the field, right where they had first landed in the red balloon.

They were so close to being home, but still had to find their way back to the house. The matchbox they had landed in was all crumpled after their crash landing, so they could no longer use it.

As Centipede stood trying to come up with an idea, he noticed a Fairy Ring of mushrooms. Of course! He could make a wish and they would be back home. He called Ladybird over to show her and explained how, when you found a Fairy Ring of mushrooms, you could make a wish and it would come true. "Go on then!" She said eagerly.

"OK then. I wish, I wish, I wish for the most magnificent flying machine there ever was to take us back home" he said, and at that, there was a flash of light and there in front of them was the most incredible flying machine they had ever seen. It looked like a space rocket with bright yellow and pink stripes. Yellow was Centipede's favourite colour and pink was Ladybird's.

Centipede eagerly climbed in and started up the engine, then helped Ladybird up into the cockpit.

"We're off" they yelled, and so they were, up-up-up and away.

That wasn't half the excitement - from up there, they could see their home.

6

The End of an Adventure

They landed in the back garden and climbed out of the flying machine. As they walked past the vegetable patch on the way to the front door, they had visions seeing Simon, excited to see them again. Instead, a wrinkly old lady opened the door to answer their knocking. When she looked to see who had knocked, she saw no one. She didn't think to look down on the doorstep where Ladybird and Centipede were. She screamed, thinking it must have been a ghost, and fainted on the spot!

Centipede thought this was hilarious, and burst out laughing, but Ladybird did not, for she had spotted the SOLD sign in the garden and realised that Simon no longer lived here, as they had moved away.

She began to cry in dismay. Centipede spotted the sign too and also started crying.

Several hours after they both finally stopped crying, Centipede had the idea that if they climbed to the top of the chimney they could look out for another house that had a

SOLD sign in the garden as that is where Simon may have moved to.

When they reached the chimney, they both started looking, but a gust of wind caught Centipede and he slipped and fell into the garden pond below. When he at last climbed back up to the chimney he was cold, wet, in a bad mood and blamed Ladybird for his fall. They were starting to give up on this idea when in the corner of his eye, something caught Centipedes attention. Another sold sign! They quickly slid down the chimney, down the roof tiles and down the drainpipe.

"Do you think it's definitely Simon's new house?" asked Ladybird. Centipede explained that he remembered overhearing Simon's mum saying that when they get back from holiday, Simon's parents would look at the house down the street as they were thinking of moving.

They left Simon's old house and walked down the road to the other house that had the sold sign out the front.
As they approached the house, Ladybird cried out "oh no, it isn't Simon's house after all".
"What makes you say that?" Centipede asked.
"Look, it's a different car in the driveway. Simon's Dad's car is red, not blue".
"Yes, you're right" said Centipede, "but I still think that this is Simon's new house and I'm going to find out" he said, sounding very determined.
They walked up the drive to a big shiny front door that had an orange wooden frame and two glass panels in it.
Centipede held his breath and knocked as loudly as he could with ten of his legs to make sure that Simon would definitely hear him.
They waited for a while and then heard footsteps approach the door. As it slowly opened, they looked up....
A tall lady stood in the doorway with a puzzled look upon her face. "Hello?" she hesitantly asked, seeing that there was no one at the door. "Is there anyone there?"
A small voice coming from the direction of her feet replied "Yes - is Simon there please?"
Still not knowing where the voice was coming from, the lady replied "Oh, err, yes he is. I'll just go and fetch him".
The lady walked away from the doorway and stood at the bottom of the stairs to call for Simon.
Simon came running down the stairs and came to the door, looking puzzled as there was no one seemingly there to greet him.
He looked up and down the street and seeing no one, began to close the door when Centipede shouted "SIMON - IT'S US! - THE LADYBIRD AND THE CENTIPEDE'.

Simon opened the door again and looked down. "Well well, what a surprise!" he said. "How on earth did you get here?"
"Well, that's a long story" both Ladybird and Centipede said.
"Come in and tell me all about it".
All afternoon, Ladybird and Centipede recounted their adventures to Simon, who sat in disbelief.
"I think I'll write a book about all of your amazing adventures" said Simon. "I will call it The Ladybird and the Centipede."

The End

7

The Story of The Ladybird and the Centipede

Staying with my Grandparents in Chorleywood, England, as a nine-year-old during the summer holidays of 1983, I decided to start writing and illustrating a book.

Over the subsequent five years, I added to the book during each summer holiday, until it was finally completed in 1988.

Somehow, years later, the tattered, pencil written book survived a move to Australia and was eventually rediscovered when I was cleaning out my garage whilst self-isolating during the Covid-19 Global Pandemic.

As a project to fill in time during this period, I decided to type up and re-illustrate the story, based on my original childhood drawings, thus giving The Ladybird and the Centipede a new lease of life, nearly forty years after their initial creation.

Philip Smith
August 2020

www.ingramcontent.com/pod-product-compliance
Lightning Source LLC
Chambersburg PA
CBHW040003110526
44587CB00001BA/36